California in the 20th Century

Nicole M. Korte

Consultants

Kristina Jovin, M.A.T.
Alvord Unified School District
Teacher of the Year

Bijan Kazerooni, M.A.
Department of History
Chapman University

Publishing Credits

Rachelle Cracchiolo, M.S.Ed., *Publisher*
Conni Medina, M.A.Ed., *Managing Editor*
Emily R. Smith, M.A.Ed., *Series Developer*
June Kikuchi, *Content Director*
Marc Pioch, M.A.Ed., and Susan Daddis, M.A.Ed., *Editors*
Courtney Roberson, *Senior Graphic Designer*

Image Credits: Cover and pp.1, 20–21 Hans Blossey/Alamy Stock Photo; p.4 (inset) Zephyr/Science Source; p.6 Movie Poster Image Art/Getty Images; p.7 (inset) Underwood Archives/Getty Images, (full page) Library of Congress [LC-USZ62-111991], (top) Archive Image/Alamy Stock Photo; pp.8–9 From the California Historical Society Collection at the University of Southern California; p.9 (top) Curt Teich Postcard Archives Heritage Images/Newscom; p.10 (bottom) Library of Congress [LC-DIG-fsa-8b26859]; p.12 Library of Congress [LC-DIG-ppprs-00226]; p.13 Library of Congress [LC-USW33-028626-C]; pp.14 (top), 29 (middle) National Archives and Records Administration [535803]; pp.14–15 Library of Congress [LC-DIG-fsa-8d31931]; p.15 (bottom) Library of Congress [LC-DIG-hec-13248]; p.17 Rue des Archives/Granger, NYC; p.18 ullstein bild/Granger, NYC; p.19 Chris Kjobech, untitled (Free Speech Movement), November 20, 1964. Watercolor on paper, 10.25 x 13 in. The Oakland Tribune Collection, the Oakland Museum of California. Gift of ANG Newspapers; p.21 Reuters/Alamy Stock Photo; p.23, (full page) PCN Photography/Alamy Stock Photo; pp.24–25 Byron Motley/Alamy Stock Photo; p.25 George Rose/Getty Images; p.27 NASA; p.31 Archive Image/Alamy Stock Photo; all other images from iStock and/or Shutterstock.

Library of Congress Cataloging-in-Publication Data

Names: Korte, Nicole M., author.
Title: California in the 20th century / Nicole M. Korte.
Description: Huntington Beach, CA : Teacher Created Materials, 2017. | Includes index. | Audience: Grade 4 to 6.
Identifiers: LCCN 2017014111 (print) | LCCN 2017014331 (ebook) | ISBN 9781425854966 (eBook) | ISBN 9781425832445 (pbk.)
Subjects: LCSH: California--History--20th century--Juvenile literature.
Classification: LCC F861.3 (ebook) | LCC F861.3 .K67 2017 (print) | DDC 979.4/053--dc23
LC record available at https://lccn.loc.gov/2017014111

Teacher Created Materials

5301 Oceanus Drive
Huntington Beach, CA 92649-1030
http://www.tcmpub.com

ISBN 978-1-4258-3244-5

© 2018 Teacher Created Materials, Inc.
Printed in China
Nordica.012019.CA21801586

Table of Contents

The Great Shake

"I was awakened from a sound sleep by the shaking of my bed and the house."

—John J. Conlon, earthquake survivor

In 1906, a major earthquake hit San Francisco. The quake lasted less than one minute. But it did a lot of damage. Buildings fell down. Fires burned around the city. Thousands of people died. About 28,000 buildings were destroyed. People had to rebuild the city.

seismograph

The Big One

The *Richter scale* measures the strength of earthquakes. The scale goes from 1 to 10. The San Francisco earthquake was the second biggest in state history. It registered a 7.8 on the Richter scale. The biggest quake was the 1857 Fort Tejon earthquake. It measured a 7.9.

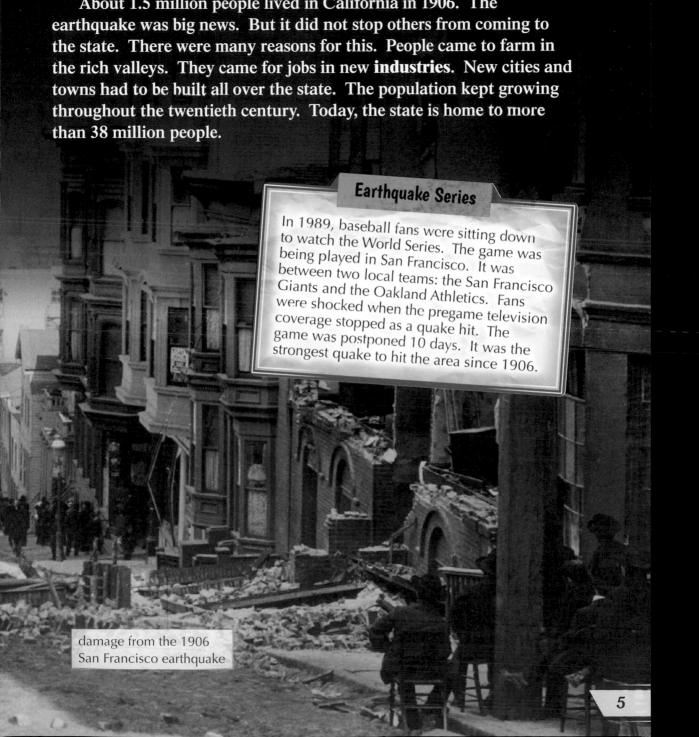

About 1.5 million people lived in California in 1906. The earthquake was big news. But it did not stop others from coming to the state. There were many reasons for this. People came to farm in the rich valleys. They came for jobs in new **industries**. New cities and towns had to be built all over the state. The population kept growing throughout the twentieth century. Today, the state is home to more than 38 million people.

Earthquake Series

In 1989, baseball fans were sitting down to watch the World Series. The game was being played in San Francisco. It was between two local teams: the San Francisco Giants and the Oakland Athletics. Fans were shocked when the pregame television coverage stopped as a quake hit. The game was postponed 10 days. It was the strongest quake to hit the area since 1906.

damage from the 1906
San Francisco earthquake

California Industries

The movie business started in New York City. But movie **producers** soon realized that Los Angeles was a great place to make movies. The weather was warm and dry. There was plenty of open space. Films could be made outside all year long. By the 1920s, studios in Hollywood made most of the movies in the world. The California movie industry became one of the largest.

More and more people came to Los Angeles to find work in films. By the end of the decade, the city had doubled in size. Over one million people lived in Los Angeles. That was a huge city for 1930! Not everyone worked in the movies. There were also new jobs in the growing oil industry. With all the new people, the city had to build new homes and transportation systems. A trolley car system was built. It made travel in the city much easier.

1925 movie poster

Silent Films

The first movies were filmed in black and white. They also had no recorded sound. Stars like Charlie Chaplin used body language and facial expressions to communicate. The theater wasn't totally silent, though. Sometimes, there was a piano or organ playing music. In some large cities, a small orchestra might be heard.

1920s movie set

In the 1920s, the famous Hollywood sign read "Hollywoodland." It remained that way until 1949 when the last four letters were removed.

HOLLYWOODLAND

Diversity Then and Now

The 1920s caused many changes. People from Mexico moved north. They wanted to live in Los Angeles. The number of Mexicans almost tripled during those 10 years. Today, people in Los Angeles come from about 180 countries.

Geography

California is a key farming state. Crops thrive in the rich soil of the Central Valley. But some areas in the state are very dry. In the 1920s, the Los Angeles **Aqueduct** brought water to areas in the southern part of the state. This allowed for more farming. During World War I, the state's farms grew enough food to feed the people of the United States and its **allies**. Farmers hoped this **boom** would last.

By 1923, more and more people farmed. The state became the main supplier of the nation's food. **Migrants** from Mexico came to work on the farms. New technology helped farmers, too. Railroad cars were refrigerated. Now, fruits and vegetables did not spoil as easily. Fresh produce could be shipped to other states.

Mexican Impact

Mexican migrants did more than work hard. They helped shape the culture of the state. Their influences can be found in language, food, art, and music.

This 1924 postcard highlights how trains helped California's citrus industry.

These workers picked berries in the early 1900s.

Depression and War

The **stock market** crashed in 1929. The years after the crash are known as the *Great Depression*. In California and elsewhere, banks lost huge amounts of money. Many banks had to close. That meant people lost their money. And there was nothing they could do about it. Other businesses closed, too. Millions of people lost their jobs. Some people were homeless and hungry. In California, more than one million people needed help and support.

Behind the Lens

Dorothea Lange studied photography in New York City. In 1918, she left the city to travel. She made money by selling her pictures. Lange ran out of money in San Francisco and decided to stay. She became well known during the Great Depression. Lange took pictures of men who were out of work in the city. Later, she was asked to take pictures of migrant families. The hope was that her photos would bring attention to their poor living conditions. *Migrant Mother* (shown below) is one of Lange's most famous photographs.

Money was not only a problem in California. During this time, the United States was hit by one of the worst **droughts** in history. Farmland dried up. Dust storms blew across the country. This time is called the *Dust Bowl*. More than two million people from the Midwest had to find new places to live. Over 200,000 of them moved to California. But the people there did not welcome the migrants. Times were hard everywhere. Many migrants took low-paying jobs to survive.

Heavy dust storms buried farm equipment. Many farmers moved to California.

The Grapes of Wrath

John Steinbeck was born in California in 1902. He worked many jobs before he became a writer. When he was 37 years old, he wrote *The Grapes of Wrath*. The book tells the story of migrants during the Great Depression. Readers at the time saw their own lives in the novel.

Geography

Recovery and Emergence

In 1933, Franklin D. Roosevelt became president. He had a plan to help people during the Great Depression. It was called the *New Deal*. Programs and laws were put in place to get people back to work. Some people built roads and bridges. Others built new schools and airports. In California, workers improved the **infrastructure**. The Central Valley Project brought water and power to the state.

During the 1940s, World War II created more jobs. The U.S. government needed supplies for the war. The country spent billions of dollars. California had a huge role in the war effort. The state produced many weapons, airplanes, and ships.

During the war, the role of women changed in California. They began to take jobs that men had always done. Women worked in factories and **shipyards**. They were crucial to the war effort. This was true across the whole country.

After World War II, California grew very quickly. New roads and houses were built. The science and technology industries thrived. These jobs drew people from across the country. The state was stronger after the war. And, it never looked back.

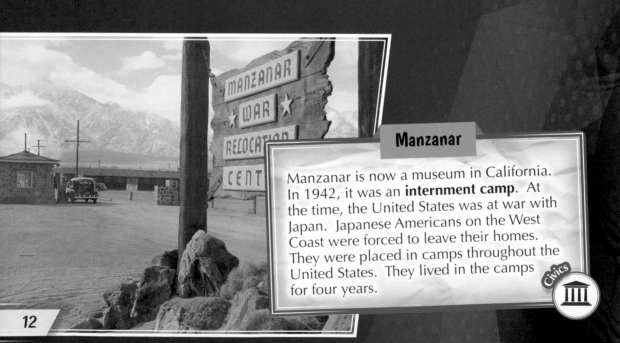

Manzanar

Manzanar is now a museum in California. In 1942, it was an **internment camp**. At the time, the United States was at war with Japan. Japanese Americans on the West Coast were forced to leave their homes. They were placed in camps throughout the United States. They lived in the camps for four years.

Rosie the Riveter

In the 1940s, women were needed in the workforce. Many men had joined the armed forces to fight in the war. The government made posters to encourage women to work. The most famous poster features "Rosie the Riveter." On the poster, she is pictured as a strong woman, ready for work. The character got her name from a 1943 song.

Economics

Two women work at an aircraft company in Long Beach.

Richmond is home to a national park. The park was built to honor all the people who worked at the shipyards. The park highlights key roles that women and African Americans played in World War II.

A female welder helps build a ship in 1943.

shipyard during World War II

DAYS ON WAY

Kaiser's Role

Henry J. Kaiser was an American **industrialist**. When World War II started, he came up with a plan. He built four large shipyards in the small city of Richmond. This city is across the bay from San Francisco. Only 23,000 people lived there at the time. But that changed. During the war, 90,000 people were hired at the shipyards. Almost one-third of the workers were women. Some African Americans were also hired. They worked in shifts. That is when groups of people worked the same job at different times during the day and night. When one person's shift ended, another person's began. This helped produce many ships for the war effort.

Kaiser supported his workers. He started health and food service programs. He even set up daycare. This was unusual at the time. Kaiser also figured out a way to build ships faster than anyone else. These shipyards made hundreds of ships for the war. Kaiser became well known because of his hard work and success.

Kaiser's Legacy

Kaiser didn't only build ships. After World War II, his company began making cars. The cars he made had **innovative** safety features. Before the war, he helped build Hoover Dam. He also started one of today's largest medical care groups, Kaiser Permanente.

Economics

HULL
No 146

Post-War California

More than 800,000 Californians served in World War II. After the war, people had to adjust to new lives. Many soldiers came back to live in the state. Their lives were very different from before the war. The state worked to help **veterans** find jobs and homes.

The state also changed because of the growing population. Soon, new cities developed. Roads, freeways, and bridges were built. People living in the cities needed schools. This growth created jobs. The state's aerospace industry also grew after the war. Many people worked in those factories. Farmland was cleared to make space for all the people moving to the state. New high-rise buildings went up. The state started to look very different from how it looked in 1941.

Aerospace

California leads the nation in many ways. One leading area is the aerospace industry. People in this industry design, build, and test all types of aircrafts. They might work with gliders, balloons, or airplanes. They even work on rockets and shuttles.

Economics

In the 1950s, more freeways around Los Angeles were built.

Societal Shift

By the 1950s, people were focused on family and fun. They spent more time with friends and family. Two theme parks opened in the state. Disneyland® opened in 1955. Sea World opened 10 years later. But change was coming. A **counterculture** began to grow. Poets, musicians, and artists led it. In California, they acted and spoke freely. They were known as the *Beat Generation*.

The 1960s was a time of **turmoil** in the United States. The Vietnam War divided the country. The civil rights movement grew across the South. California was at the center of a free speech movement. People felt angry about injustices in the world. They spoke out. Many of them settled in San Francisco. Their long hair and clothes made them stand out. They were called *hippies*.

Disneyland

Since its opening, Disneyland has become one of the biggest employers in the area. There were 1,280 workers on opening day. In 10 years, that number more than tripled. In 2001, the park grew to include a second park. Together, they **employ** tens of thousands of people.

Students **protest** at the University of California, Berkeley, in 1964.

Silicon Valley

The Santa Clara Valley is in the northern part of the state. It is better known as *Silicon Valley*. San Jose is the biggest city in the area. Silicon is an element. It is used to make computer chips. That is how the valley got its nickname. The valley has been the hub of technology since the 1970s.

Eyes in the Sky

Satellites are machines that circle Earth. They gather data for scientists to study. California companies play a huge role in producing these "eyes in the sky." Six out of ten of all satellites in the world are made in the state. And one out of five commercial satellites are launched from there.

Economics

Silicon Valley

In 1976, Steve Jobs started a company called Apple®. It is in Silicon Valley. The first computer Apple released looked like a typewriter. But it changed the world. More companies joined the tech boom. Soon, the valley was filled with **start-ups**. Very few start-ups changed the world in the way that Apple did.

Then, Google® and Yahoo!® arrived in the 1990s. Technology has been growing since. Today, the valley is home to thousands of high-tech firms.

Googleplex

Googleplex is the name of Google's world headquarters. Workers there enjoy unusual extras. The company provides bikes to get around the campus. There are also areas where people can take naps!

napping pods at Google

Sports and Entertainment

California has many theme parks. The state is home to famous movie stars. People can find beautiful beaches. More than three hundred days a year are sunny. There are many things to do and see in the state. Starting in the 1980s, sports and music took center stage.

Sports

California sports teams have always been popular. There are a lot of people in the state to be fans! The San Francisco 49ers were one of the best football teams in the 1980s. The star of the team was Joe Montana. The team won four Super Bowls in 10 years. In Los Angeles, the "Showtime" Lakers entertained. The team was led by Earvin "Magic" Johnson Jr. and Kareem Abdul-Jabbar. Baseball teams in the state won three World Series championships in the '80s.

In 1984, the world focused on Los Angeles. The city hosted the Summer Olympics. Americans did well in the games. Carl Lewis won four gold medals in track and field. Mary Lou Retton won gold in gymnastics. She received two perfect scores!

West Coast Baseball

There were no major league baseball teams on the West Coast until 1957. That year, the state got two teams. The Brooklyn Dodgers moved to Los Angeles. And the New York Giants moved to San Francisco. Today, there are five baseball teams in the state!

Geography

In 1984, the city of Los Angeles was excited and honored to host the Olympics.

Basketball Legend

Kareem Abdul-Jabbar is one of the best basketball players of all time. He is best known for the 15 years he played with the Los Angeles Lakers. Today, Abdul-Jabbar spends his time giving back. He is a sponsor of the Skyhook Foundation. This group works with the L.A. Unified School District to send students to Camp Skyhook. This weeklong camp provides hands-on learning in science and math.

Music

Each year, music lovers go to concerts. They listen to the radio. And they buy a lot of music. People download songs in only a few minutes today. In the 1990s, music came on compact discs (CDs). CDs improved the sound quality of music. Cassette tapes did not sound very clear. Vinyl records were even worse. Music today sounds clearer than ever before.

The music and bands of the state show how diverse California is. Hip-hop music started in New York. But its popularity on the West Coast grew. Rappers in the state infused their lyrics with their local sounds and cultures. Indie rock also became popular. Many people created the sounds of the Golden State.

California Music Festivals

Some big music events are held in California. Coachella is the most well known. It began in 1999 and featured lesser-known artists and bands. Since then, it has become a stage for big pop stars. Stagecoach is also a music event held in the state. This country music festival started in 2007.

Many Californians enjoy going to music festivals.

Power Tower

Capitol Records is a music company. It started in Los Angeles during the 1940s. Many bands work with the company. It is based in a special building. The building is a Hollywood **landmark**.

Leading the Way

The state of California and its people are leaders in many areas. They lead in farming and technology. They lead in sports and business. The state is also paving the way in **conservation**. State leaders have made laws to protect nature. They push for programs to recycle. And they promote saving energy and water. All the effort is paying off. Pollution and waste have been reduced in the state.

California Condors

California condors are on the endangered species list. In the 1970s, only a few dozen were left in the wild. By 1987, the number was down to 10. A plan was put in place to save them. Condors were bred in zoos. In 1992, some condors were released into the wild. As of 2014, over 400 condors live in the wild or in zoos.

Wind farms help reduce pollution.

California is a special place to live or visit. The twentieth century changed the state in many ways. People in the state farmed. They built ships and cars. Then, they made rockets and planes. And, there was always music and movies. What a diverse state!

Teacher in Space

Barbara Morgan was born in Fresno. She was the first teacher to carry out a mission in space. For 24 years, she taught elementary school in the United States, as well as Ecuador. Then, in 1998, NASA chose her to be an Educator Astronaut. Morgan's first flight in space was in 2007. She put in over 300 hours in space. She retired from NASA the next year.

Scrapbook It!

In the twentieth century, California grew in many areas. People immigrated to the state from all over the world. After the Great Depression and World War II, other industries joined farming to make the state's economy grow. Technology boomed in Silicon Valley. Sports and entertainment continued to play big roles in the state.

Choose five events from the twentieth century. Pick things that you believe were most important to California during the last century. Design a scrapbook page for each with at least one picture. Be sure to explain why you chose each event.

Glossary

allies—countries that join together for a common cause or goal

aqueduct—a human-made canal that brings water from one place to another

boom—a period of growth, progress, or sudden expansion

conservation—the protection of natural resources for later use

counterculture—a culture whose values and morals are different from those followed by most people

droughts—periods of dry weather

employ—to hire someone for a job

industrialist—a person who owns or manages a company

industries—groups of businesses that work together to provide particular products or services

infrastructure—basic framework for industry in a state

innovative—using new or exciting ideas

internment camp—a place people are forced to relocate to

landmark—an object or structure that is easy to see and can serve as a guide to mark a location

migrants—people who move from one place to another in search of work

producers—people who oversee and help pay for performances

protest—to show disagreement of something

shipyards—places where ships are built and fixed

start-ups—new businesses

stock market—the place where stocks and bonds are bought and sold

turmoil—a state of confusion or chaos

veterans—people who have served in the military for their country during a time of war

Index

Your Turn!

Plan Ahead

People who live in California must be ready for earthquakes at any time. They should have emergency kits prepared.

Think of all the necessary tools, supplies, and other materials that might be needed after a major earthquake. On a large sheet of paper, design and illustrate an emergency kit for you and your family. Use labels and captions to give reasons why you included these items. If you have pets, be sure to include their needs!